W9-AXE-474

PLANET EARTH

Truth Is Stranger than Fiction

NEWS

Presents

SUPER HUMANS

Written by **Keltie Thomas**
Illustrated by **Greg Hall**

MAPLE TREE PRESS

Maple Tree Press Inc.
51 Front Street East, Suite 200, Toronto, Ontario M5E 1B3
www.mapletreepress.com

Distributed in Canada by Raincoast Books
9050 Shaughnessy Street, Vancouver, British Columbia V6P 6E5

Distributed in the United States by Publishers Group West
1700 Fourth Street, Berkeley, California 94710

Dedication
For my Dad—a.k.a. Dr. Deviatsky—who has perfected the art
of going ape

Cataloguing in Publication Data
Thomas, Keltie
      Planet earth news presents : super humans / Keltie Thomas ;
illustrations by Greg Hall.

(Planet earth news)
Includes index.
ISBN-13 978-1-897066-51-5 (bound) / ISBN-10 1-897066-51-1 (bound)
ISBN-13 978-1-897066-52-2 (pbk.) / ISBN-10 1-897066-52-X (pbk.)

      1. History--Miscellanea--Juvenile literature. 2. Curiosities and
wonders--Juvenile literature. I. Hall, Greg, 1963-   II. Title.
III. Title: Super humans. IV. Series.

AG243.T399 2006   j081   C2005-904645-7

Design, art direction & illustration: Greg Hall

We acknowledge the financial support of the Canada Council for the Arts,
the Ontario Arts Council, the Government of Canada through the Book
Publishing Industry Development Program (BPIDP), and the Government
of Ontario through the Ontario Media Development Corporation's Book
Initiative for our publishing activities.

ONTARIO ARTS COUNCIL
CONSEIL DES ARTS DE L'ONTARIO

Printed in China

A   B   C   D   E   F

Acknowledgments
Special thanks to the Ontario Arts
Council, all the wonderful people at
Maple Tree Press, especially Sheba,
Anne, and Victoria, and Greg Hall
whose fabulous art makes these
pages come alive.

Contents

EARTHLINGS

Humans are creatures of invention who have risen up to rule the world. Today, nearly 6.5 billion human beings inhabit the Earth and our numbers are growing. We've spread to each and every continent and corner of the globe, invading other creatures' turf along the way. What's more, our inventions, such as electric power, wheels, and the telephone, have radically changed life here on Earth for better or for worse. And that's exactly what makes Earthlings so extraordinary.

There are no creatures we know of any place in the universe quite like the humans who live on Earth. What other creatures do you know who can trace their family tree back to a sponge and invent a mirror to look into the future? What other creatures are fashion animals that wear smart clothes? Or flock to buy pet rocks? Or build computers to take over the world? Turn the page for the inside scoop on how the life of humans is stranger than fiction.

Are Extraordinary

Spot the
Hoax Busters

Keep your wits about you as you read this book. Earthlings have been known to exaggerate to tell a good story and some love to pull tricks, or hoaxes, that fool fellow Earthlings. Use the Hoax Busters throughout this book to develop your sense of phony baloney. Consider each scene under the magnifying glass by asking yourself questions such as: Could the phenomenon be caused by other means or forces? If so, which ones? Check your answers on page 63 and keep score to see how you rate as a Hoax Buster.

Tales That Got Us

We're All a Bunch of Monkeys

Shocking! No way! Outrageous! That's what people roared in the 1800s, when naturalist Charles Darwin concluded that humans evolved from apes. Despite the uproar, Darwin's theory launched a search for the "missing link" between humans and apes.

In 1912, scientists found skull and jawbone fragments near Piltdown, England. They claimed that the large, humanlike brain-case and apelike jawbone came from a human who

Meet the Piltdowns.

had lived half a million years ago—the missing link. But not all scientists agreed.

As fossils of early humans continued to turn up, scientists couldn't put the pieces of the human evolution puzzle together. Piltdown Man just didn't fit.

In 1953, tests revealed that Piltdown Man's skull was less than 50,000 years old and his jawbone belonged to a modern orangutan. Piltdown Man was a hoax! The phony fossil led scientists down the wrong track for over 40 years as they tried to sketch out a picture of human evolution to include it.

What's the difference between apes and monkeys? Apes have no tail like monkeys do and a brain that's twice as big.

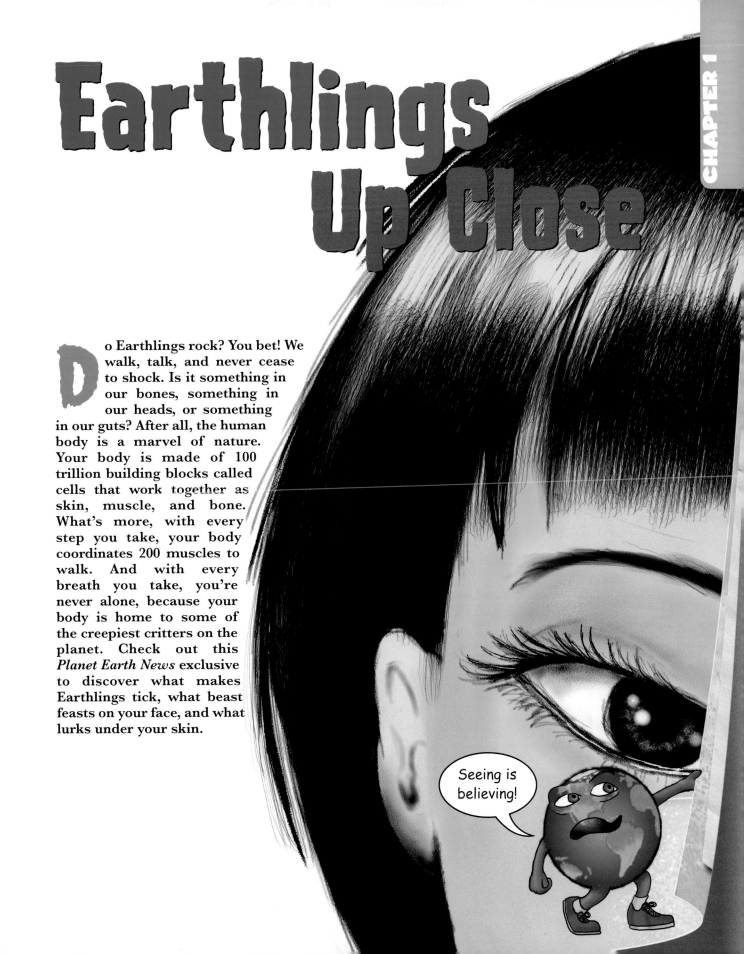

CHAPTER 1

Earthlings Up Close

Do Earthlings rock? You bet! We walk, talk, and never cease to shock. Is it something in our bones, something in our heads, or something in our guts? After all, the human body is a marvel of nature. Your body is made of 100 trillion building blocks called cells that work together as skin, muscle, and bone. What's more, with every step you take, your body coordinates 200 muscles to walk. And with every breath you take, you're never alone, because your body is home to some of the creepiest critters on the planet. Check out this *Planet Earth News* exclusive to discover what makes Earthlings tick, what beast feasts on your face, and what lurks under your skin.

Seeing is believing!

Earthlings Exposed

Hey, Earthling! Did you know you have stars in your eyes, a skeleton, er, sponge in your closet, and aliens crawling under your skin? Get the inside scoop.

You're Star Material, Kiddo

OK, you may not be the next big rock star. Nevertheless, you are made of stardust from the stars that sparkle in the sky. Your skin and bones and all the other parts of your body are made of elements, such as carbon, oxygen, and nitrogen, which are forged inside stars. But it may not be as glamorous as it sounds, because stars release these elements when they belch. Burp! At its core, a star is like a hot furnace burning fuel, which makes it shine. As a large star's core gets hotter, it forms carbon and other elements—the building blocks of all matter in the universe. Eventually, the star explodes (called a supernova), belching the elements into space as dust. Maybe Earthlings should be called Burpees!

A Squishy Relative

Would you believe an ancient sea sponge might be your great (to the millionth generation) uncle? Sound far-fetched? Scientists believe that all Earth's creatures, including human beings, have evolved from a single ancient organism. What's more, recent research reveals that sea sponges may have been the first animals to inhabit Earth. When scientist Mitchell Sogin wanted to know what the first animal looked like, he used computers to trace the development of the world's oldest species, such as jellyfish, sponges, sea anemones, and starfish, back to a common ancestor. Lo and behold—a sponge popped up! The sponge is the earliest known animal made of more than one cell. Scientists think that the ability to grow more than one type of cell launched animals down a path of development, or evolution, that led to the rise of humans. Who knew sponges had it in them?

EXPOSED!

Put a sea sponge through a sieve and it breaks apart into bits. But in a few hours, it will regroup back into an exact copy of the original sponge. No other living thing can come back to life like this!

Hoax Busters

HUMANS BECOME COMPUTER NETWORKS

If a high-tech company gets its way, the human body will become a computer network. The company says it will use human skin to network personal gadgets together, such as a cell phone, PDA, watch, and music player.

Is this ...
A) an April Fools' joke?
B) phony baloney?
C) for real?
D) an idea only a human could think up?

Answers on page 63.

MICROSCOPIC VIEW

Aliens Lurk under Your Skin

Pssst. Don't hit the panic button, but you are outnumbered by aliens at this very moment. And there's just no getting away from them...because they live under your skin! They're microscopic organisms called bacteria. Believe it or not, more than 500 different kinds of bacteria make themselves at home in the human body. The little aliens hang out in your gut, for example, where they make up trillions of cells. In fact, these "alien cells" outnumber the human cells in your body. While the bacteria in your gut help convert food into energy, others help protect you from disease, and still others may invade your body and make you ill. Scientists say that by studying how bacteria interact with the body we may be able to find better cures for diseases.

Walk Like an Earthling

Check out how evolution equipped modern-day humans to walk on two legs hands-free and carry a big brain.

Earthlings
Rise Up and March

What moved them to do it no one knows. But six million years ago, the ancestors of modern-day Earthlings rose up from all fours and began walking on two legs. It was a radical move. It set them apart from their relatives, the apes, and all the other creatures on Earth, but walking upright was less stable than all other ways of getting around. Walking on two legs demanded coordination and the work of many muscles. So why take the step? Scientists think it may have enabled *Homo erectus*, a.k.a. upright man, to spot predators and prey at a distance or keep his head above water during floods. Whatever the case may have been, walking upright left the hands free, which paved the way for the evolution of modern-day humans. How's that for starting a revolution?

Couch Potatoes
Born to Run

Hey, couch potatoes! When it comes to getting some exercise, you've got no more excuses. According to recent research, your body, and that of all modern-day humans, is well adapted for running marathons. Some scientists think that running long distances may have given the first beings who rose up on two legs more of an edge than walking. They say the ability to run great distances may have allowed early Earthlings to rule the plains of Africa. Although early humans couldn't sprint nearly as fast as many animals, they could go the distance to reach the leftovers of animal carcasses before scavenging animals arrived.

EXPOSED!

The average human being walks 22,531 km (14,000 mi.) during his or her lifetime and spends a total of five years eating and drinking to fuel up that body to walk the walk, think, and handle tools.

Earthlings

Finally Get a Grip

Walking on two legs freed up the hands of early Earthlings to get a grip on the world. Suddenly, they were able to carry babies, food, weapons, or tools in their hands, and eventually their hands became extremely nimble. They used the "power grip" of the inner hand to get a firm grasp on rocks, branches, simple tools, and the like. They also evolved a long, mobile thumb that enabled them to develop the "precision grip"—the ability to hold, say, a pen between the thumb and index finger for writing. No other creature on Earth, including humans' closest relatives chimpanzees, can do such operations as delicately as humans can. This deftness enabled early Earthlings to make and use fine tools, giving them an "upper hand" in evolution.

The Bionic Truth

In the 1970s, the adventures of the *Six Million Dollar Man* and the *Bionic Woman* mesmerized kids everywhere. The TV show characters each had a bionic arm, legs, and eye or ear that looked and worked exactly like real body parts except for one major detail. The bionics gave the characters superhuman strength! Now scientists have developed real-world bionics, but they don't look and work like those of the TV characters. An experimental bionic suit, which people strap onto their legs and wear as a backpack, gives people superhuman strength to carry heavy loads over long distances. Other bionics replace lost limbs. In 2003, 13-year-old Kat Reid, who lost a leg to bone cancer, received the world's first bionic leg that mimics natural growth. Since then, she's been able to walk normally.

Upper Hand Swells Earthlings' Heads

Once early Earthlings got a free hand, it went straight to their heads. No kidding! As they used their hands to fashion and manipulate precise tools, they nudged their brains, which controlled the tools, to develop hand in hand with their handy forelimbs. Over millions of years, the human brain doubled in size. Today, the skull of modern-day humans is shaped like a dome to hold one of the biggest brains on the planet. And many scientists think it's the cleverest. The human brain functions like a computer. It receives information from the eyes, ears, nose, hands, and mouth and processes it to send messages to parts of the body to control balance and movement and enable people to think, understand, and remember. In fact, scientists call modern-day Earthlings *Homo sapiens*, meaning "wise man."

What's Eating You?

So what's eating you, Earthling? Could it be the fact that you're never alone? Could it be the tiny mites, bugs, and bacteria that suck your blood and call your body home?

Beast Has a Feast
on Your Face

An eight-legged "beast" has a daily feast on the skin on your face. But have no fear. Even though this voracious freeloader looks like a worm armed with small claws and needlelike mouthparts, it's quite harmless. Phew! It makes itself at home on most people. And it's so tiny that it could fit on the period at the end of this sentence along with three of its face-feasting pals. The miniscule mite crawls headfirst into a follicle, or pore, in your skin to gorge on dead skin cells and bacteria. It's called a follicle mite, and it has cousins that hang out and picnic in the follicles of your hair and your eyelashes. Maybe picky eating runs in their family, because you won't find any of these mites on any other creatures on Earth!

Lice Want
Your Blood

Do head lice have a thing for young blood? No one can tell for sure. But the wingless little insects tend to crawl into the hair of kids to feed. About the size of sesame seeds, head lice are visible to the naked eye. Even so, if the little bloodsuckers hunker down in your hair one day, you may not notice them until your scalp becomes itchy from their bites. The "lousy" pests will pierce your scalp and suck your blood through sharp tube-shaped mouthparts. What's more, they'll inject spit, or saliva, which is what makes the bites itch. And they'll keep sucking until they've drunk their fill. Talk about bloodthirsty. The good news is that you can get rid of lice with medicated shampoo and a fine-tooth comb, which will remove the eggs they glue to your hair.

Critters on page are **larger** than life.

You've "Gutta" Love 'Em

Bacteria, the microscopic organisms that live on and under your skin (see page 9), love your guts. Hundreds of different kinds of these tiny microbes stake out territory in the large intestine of your digestive system and live there. Unlike bacteria that cause disease, the bacteria in your gut are friendly bugs. Some scientists think that in exchange for the regular meals they help themselves to in your gut, some of them break down indigestible foods into sugars, vitamins, and other substances your body can absorb. Recent research also shows that some of these bacteria may help your gut develop the blood vessels you need to absorb nutrients. Is that gutsy, or what?!

MICROSCOPIC VIEW

Earworms Play with Your Mind

Ever had a catchy song or tune pop into your head and refuse to go away? It happens to 98 percent of people. One scientist calls these songs "earworms." Most earworms disappear on their own after an hour, but some can hang around for a whole day.

Vampires Hide Out under the Bed

Bed bugs have been lurking in the sleeping quarters of Earthlings for thousands of years. The brownish pea-size critters are like miniature vampires. They live on blood, feed only at night, and hide out during the day, crawling on six legs into cracks, crevices, walls, ceilings, floors, and even mattresses. But chances are you've never seen one because, until recently, they were all but wiped out in North America. The notorious bloodsuckers bite humans without waking them then drink up for as long as 15 minutes. The poor victims don't feel anything until long after the bugs have made their getaway. After that, the bug bites can be painful and itchy for up to a week. Ouch!

The Case of the Toad-Vomiting Woman

Got a frog in your throat? If you'd asked Catharina Geisslerin that in 1642, you'd have been wise to run for cover. Chances are she'd have opened her mouth and showered you with toad vomit to prove it.

Catharina said that she had swallowed tadpoles while swimming and ever since then toads hopped inside her gut. Doctors made house calls to investigate. But as she continued to vomit fully grown toads and frogs the doctors failed to uncover any other explanation.

The case of the toad-vomiting woman remained unsolved throughout her life. Of course, that may have been because Catharina mysteriously stopped vomiting anytime a doctor examined her.

Once she died, doctors rushed to dissect her body. Much to their surprise, they found no trace of frogs or toads in her stomach. What no one knew back then was that the stomach's digestive juices would have quickly wiped them out. Catharina must have swallowed full-grown amphibians and vomited them shortly after to keep up the spectacular ruse. How's that for a sick trick?

Blecch, ribbit, hop!

According to Guinness World Records, in 1988, Kevin Cole of New Mexico blew a piece of spaghetti 19 cm (7½ in.) out of his nose in a single blow. Yuck!

CHAPTER 2

Mummies Scare Up the Dead

Are Earthlings born to rot? Maybe not. But as soon as they die, their bodies start to break down. *Planet Earth News* kids you not! The microbes, or bacteria, living on people's skin and deep within their gut begin gobbling up muscle, fat, and everything else in sight. Within days, the skin turns green, the fingernails and toenails fall off, and the rotting flesh gives off a foul odor. P-U!

What's more, long before the dead create such a big stink, flesh flies, blow flies, and beetles can detect their smell. The insects pick up the whiff as if it were an invitation to a dinner party.

Nevertheless, people all over the world have found ways to outwit these ravenous scavengers, preserving the flesh of the dead, turning dead bodies into mummies. And sometimes sand, ice, and bogs prevent dead bodies from decaying, creating natural mummies. Meet some mummies in this *Planet Earth News* exclusive and discover the tales their ancient flesh scare up today.

Mu...mu...mummy?!

Tales from the Crypt

Nowadays, mummies are a bit like celebrities. They don't get out much without attracting a crowd and some even wear the latest designer fashions. Check out mummies' cryptic lives.

Mummy Heads Up
Meetings

Drop by University College London, in England, and you might bump into a mummy in broad daylight. The mummy of famous British thinker, or philosopher, Jeremy Bentham shows itself there every day.

When Bentham died in 1832, he left his body to science. In his will, he wrote instructions for his body to be dissected, preserved, then displayed at the college. But his mummified head ended up looking so gruesome that his friends replaced it with a wax one. Then they dressed his skeletal remains in his old coat and breeches, sat him in a chair on display, and tucked his mummified head between his feet. Rumor has it that college staff wheel Bentham's mummy around to attend regular college meetings.

Honey, I Shrunk the Heads!

Once upon a time, many people could have made this claim without joking at all. People all over the planet have preserved the heads of ancestors and shrunk the heads of enemies as war prizes. The Jivaro Indians of Ecuador were skilled headhunters, for example. They cut off the heads of slain enemies and shrunk them to the size of a fist. The Jivaro's head-shrinking method even kept their enemies' facial features intact. They peeled off the skin, sewed shut the eyes and mouth, then boiled the resulting sack and filled it with hot rocks and sand. The Jivaro believed that preserving their enemies' heads this way allowed them to possess their enemies' power. Heady stuff!

Mummies Swap Bandages for "Plastic Wrap"

Imagine a mummy going bump in the night. Chances are you pictured an ancient Egyptian mummy wrapped in bandages from head to toe. Egyptians preserved the dead like this thousands of years ago, because they believed their bodies would come back to life in a world beyond death. They removed the brain and internal organs, painted the body with oily resin, and wrapped it in linen. But nowadays, Dr. Gunther von Hagens leaves organs intact, swaps linen bandages for revealing "plastic wrap," and preserves the dead in action poses. Take *The Runner* preserved by von Hagens, for example. *The Runner* stands tall in full stride, showing off his muscles, bones, and blood vessels. Von Hagens uses plastination, a technique he invented that transforms body tissues into lifelike plastic. What's more, he displays preserved bodies in exhibitions worldwide to give people a glimpse at the inner workings of the human body. Now that's something that could really get under a person's skin!

Frozen Mummy Wakes Up in the Future

Woman dies, has her physical body preserved in a deep freeze, then comes back to life thousands of years in the future. Sound like something that could only happen in the movies? Not if some people get their wish. They hope that one day cryogenics—the science of preserving body tissues at extremely low temperatures—will find a way to bring frozen dead bodies back to life. So once they die, these cryogenics believers are having their bodies frozen and stored in special cryogenic chambers that look like giant steel thermoses. Nevertheless, most scientists agree that the day science can revive any of those who are frozen is a long, long way off and many think it's highly unlikely to ever come.

King Tut Goes for a Checkup

Until 2004, it had been 35 years since anyone had seen the 3,300-year-old mummy of the Egyptian boy-king who died in his teens. In 1968, archeologists (scientists who study evidence of our past) X-rayed King Tutankhamen's mummy for clues to his untimely death. Some scientists believed the results pointed to foul play. In 2004, archeologists ran tests with more advanced equipment. They roused Tut from his tomb and moved him into a van that held a portable coffin-sized CT scanner. The resulting 3-D picture of Tut's skull ruled out a violent death, but didn't reveal how he died. And Tut's not talking.

TUT MOBILE

Natural-Born Mummies

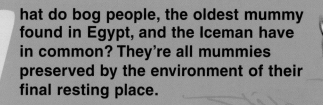

hat do bog people, the oldest mummy found in Egypt, and the Iceman have in common? They're all mummies preserved by the environment of their final resting place.

Belle of the Bog

When two men accidentally fished a dead body out of a peat bog near Yde, Netherlands, in 1897, they took one look and lit out. The corpse looked like an old hag. The peat in the bog had preserved the dead woman's flesh, turning it brown and withered like a dried prune. Her eyes were screwed shut, her teeth as black as tar, and thick locks of red hair covered only half her head. But eventually the men got the nerve to return and inform authorities of their discovery. Scientists rushed to examine the body. The scientists noticed that her feet were the size of a child's, so she hadn't been an old woman when she died but a young girl. They named her Yde Girl, and she went to the Drents Museum for display. But what had she looked like? To find out, the museum curator had a medical artist use CT scans of her skull and computers to create a 3-D model of her head. And the artist's work revealed a drop-dead beauty!

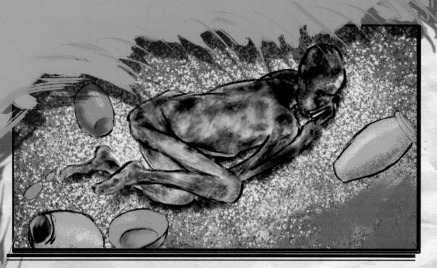

Old Mummy Is No Dummy

The oldest mummy found in Egypt goes by the nickname Ginger, thanks to his bright red hair. And he's no dummy, er, human-made mummy. Nature made the mummy about 5,200 years ago—more than 1,000 years before the Egyptians began practicing artificial mummification. Archeologists discovered Ginger curled up among pots, tools, and jewelry in a shallow desert grave at Gebelein, Egypt. The hot, dry sand of the grave had dried out his dead body and mummified it. As the sand absorbed all the water and fluids in his body, it robbed the microbes that decay flesh of their breeding ground and place to go to work. So Ginger's flesh remained well preserved for thousands of years. Even the mummy's fingernails and toenails were found intact!

EXPOSED!

One time, a frozen mummy of a bison that lived 200,000 years ago melted out of ice. But before scientists could save it, wolves ate it. Now that's well-preserved meat!

MUMMIES CRACK COLD CASE

In the 1980s, mummies helped scientists crack a cold case more than 100 years old. The mummies provided evidence that solved the mystery of what killed the men on the Franklin Expedition to the Arctic in the 1840s.

Is this a...

A) likely story?
B) case of mummies coming back from the dead?
C) case of dead bodies telling tales without talking?
D) true story?

Answers on page 63.

Iceman Comes in from the Cold

One fine September day in 1991, a frozen corpse popped out of a melting glacier in the Tyrolean Alps between Austria and Italy. The body was so well preserved that when two mountain climbers stumbled across it, they assumed the Iceman was a victim of a recent climbing accident. Little did they realize the human remains were more than 5,000 years old! Cold, dry air had mummified the Iceman's body, preventing microbes from decaying it before it became trapped in the ice, where it lay for thousands of years. The Iceman's clothes, one shoe, backpack, tools, weapons, and food also remained intact. And they helped reveal that he had lived and died during the late Stone Age. The Iceman also carried a copper ax, bow and arrows, and a fire-starting kit. Recently, X-rays revealed a stone arrowhead stuck in his left shoulder. One scientist estimates that the painful wound killed the Iceman in three to ten hours. Who knew it would take thousands of years for him to come in from the cold!

presents **Tales That Got Us**

Mummy's Curse
Kills Tomb Disturbers

When Howard Carter and Lord Carnarvon discovered King Tutankhamen's tomb in Egypt in 1922, the British press had a field day. Newspapers ran stories about the "Curse of King Tut." And when Lord Carnarvon suddenly died a few months later, many people believed the curse had struck him down. Rumor soon flew around the world that all those who had entered the tomb were mysteriously dying one by one.

But the facts of the matter weren't nearly as

Who goes there?

intriguing. First off, there was no curse of King Tut inscribed on the tomb. The press had invented the curse to tell a good story. Secondly, Lord Carnarvon's death was no mystery. He cut a mosquito bite open while he was shaving and the bite became infected. Without medicine available, the infection killed him. Thirdly, of the 26 people who were in the tomb when the burial chamber was opened, only 6 were dead 12 years later. And Carter, the lead "tomb disturber," kicked around for another 17 years.

Twelve researchers opened King Casimir's tomb in Poland, in 1973, and shortly after ten of them died. One of the survivors later discovered that the "mummy's curse" was toxic fungus in the tomb.

CHAPTER 3

Fashion, Fads, and the Naked Ape

Ever heard human beings called the naked ape? Well, it's not true. Even though we humans have much less body hair than our closest living relatives, the great apes, hair covers almost every inch of our skin. Scientists think we have body hair because we've evolved from hairy creatures. But just how or why we've lost a lot of it over time is a mystery.

What is known is that people spend a lot of time fussing, messing, and obsessing with the hair we do have—especially the hair on our heads. We cut, curl, and style our locks to keep up with the latest trends, maintain our "mane," fit in with "the gang," and express ourselves. Comb through the naked truth about hair, find out what makes people fashion animals, and get to the root of why we follow the craziest fads in this *Planet Earth News* exclusive.

Follow the herd!

The Naked Truth

Whether we have bad hair days or good hair days, humans definitely lead hairy lives. Here are the details—detangled.

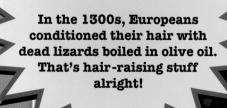

Meet the Hairy Bunch

Say, just say, aliens made a TV show about Earthlings. Maybe they would call it *The Hairy Bunch*. That's because the average human being (you) is covered with hair. Short, fine hairs cover all of your skin except for the palms of your hands, soles of your feet, and your lips. Longer hairs sprout out of your head. What's more, hair grows circles and lines around your eyes, a.k.a. your eyelashes and eyebrows, and even grows right up your nose. Sound gross? All these types of hair do special jobs for you. The hair on your skin helps keep your body warm. Your eyebrows help keep sweat from dripping into your eyes. Your eyelashes trigger your eyelids to close when specks of dust hit them. And those hairs up your nose? Well, they help keep out the dust, bugs, and whatever else flies in on the nosey express.

STYLIST WANTED FOR HAIRY TIMES AHEAD

The hair on the human head is dead, because hair cells die as they reach the surface of the scalp. But that doesn't stop hair from making waves. Check out this gallery of trend-setting hairstyles through the ages.

Blondes Have More Wigs

The Look: A wig of tight blonde curls shaped like sausages
Worn By: Ancient Roman women

Shave Like an Egyptian

The Look: A clean-shaven dome head
Worn By: Ancient Egyptians for the ease of wearing wigs and men in the 90s for a slick bald look

Mountain 'Do

The Look: A mountain of hair stuffed with miniature ships, gardens, waterfalls, and butterflies
Worn By: European women of the 1700s

The Original Punk Rocker

The Look: Blue, purple, pink, and yellow powdered wigs
Worn By: British men in the late 1700s

The Beehive

The Look: First came the Beehive, teased hair piled "mile high," then came the "anti-hive," hair ironed perfectly straight
Worn By: Women in the 1960s

The Mohawk

The Look: A shaved head with a spiky ridge of hair sticking up in the middle
Worn By: 1600s Iroquois warriors, 70s punk rockers, and 2000s sports stars

Fashion Rules

Do clothes make the human? Check out how people dress for success, make statements with clothes, and flock to follow fads.

What a Fashion Animal!

So you're a human. You're a warm-blooded creature also known as a mammal. But unlike most mammals, you don't have a thick coat of fur to keep yourself warm and protect your skin from the elements. What do you do? Dress up like an animal. Stone Age humans wore animal furs and skins for warmth and protection. At some point, people also began wearing animal furs and skins for the appearance and qualities animals possess. Around 3000 B.C., for example, Egyptian hunters attached a wolf tail to their grass skirts, for the wolf's strength, swiftness, and ferocity. Today, people the world over wear fur, feathers, and leather from animals as well as fake fur and leather. But refusing to wear the fur off an animal's back is also a popular fashion statement.

Jeans Full of Beans

Pssst. You know those jeans you're wearing? They're no ordinary pair of pants. Know any other pants that are made of fabric that's hundreds of years old, yet never goes out of style? Jeans are made of indigo blue denim. In the 1600s, the French wove denim from wool and silk. And in 1872, modern jeans were born when Jacob Davis and Levi Strauss reinforced the seams of denim pants with copper rivets for goldminers. In the 1950s, wearing jeans became a symbol of a rebel when movie stars wore them on the silver screen to portray tough characters living on the fringe. So many schools banned them, but that only made jeans more popular. Who knew jeans were so full of beans?

Human Flock Buys Pet Rocks

Monkey see, monkey do. When it comes to fads that old saying just may be true. When the hula hoop rolled into the world in 1957, for example, people snapped it up in record numbers. Twenty-five million people stampeded stores to get one in the first few months and more than 75 million followed in their footsteps. If you think that's loopy, people also flocked to buy pet rocks! In 1975, businessman Gary Dahl stuck a plain old rock in a cardboard box with a "training manual." Dahl billed the rock as the perfect pet, because it never made a mess, misbehaved, or needed a walk. And people bought up one million pet rocks in five months flat. Sound crazy? It was. Today, pet rocks often get top billing as the world's most ridiculous fad.

Strange BUT True

Nutty for Putty

When a magazine ran a story about Silly Putty in 1950, a quarter million orders for the bouncing goo rolled in in just three days. Silly Putty became a fad, then a classic toy. In fact, astronauts on the 1968 *Apollo 8* mission took the nutty putty to the Moon.

EXPOSED!

Andrew Fischer became known as The Forehead Guy in 2005, when he sold his forehead as ad space for $37, 375. Who knew empty skin could be so profit-full!

Human Feet Sneak Around

When it comes to outfitting human feet, sneakers have all the competition beat. The popular footwear strolled into the world in the late 1800s, sporting canvas tops and rubber soles. And it wasn't long before the shoe became a trendsetter, constantly morphing style and shape for design and performance. In 1918, for example, high-top canvas sneakers appeared with a protective ankle patch and treads designed to give basketball players more traction. Platform sneakers with soles a few centimetres high raised people to new heights in the 1960s. In the 1970s, the Earth Shoe, a trend-setting sneaker with a heel lower than the toe, brought people back down to Earth. In the 1990s, sneakers with high-tech foam springs built into the sole put "boing" in people's steps. And today, sneakers run around the world sporting new styles and designs every few months.

Smart Clothes

What does a creature of fashion do with a big brain? Design smart clothes! Check out the "smarty pants," talking bags, and thinking shoes smart people have designed.

No More Dirty Laundry

Imagine this: you ride your bike through a gigantic mud puddle and mud splashes all over your buddy's white pants. But instead of soaking up the mud, his "smarty pants" clean it away until the mud completely disappears. One day, smart clothes like this may exist beyond your imagination. Recently, researchers invented a smart fabric that cleans itself without washing. When the researchers coated cotton fabric with the chemical titanium dioxide, sunlight reacted with the coating to break down dirt on the surface. So the researchers hope to make self-cleaning clothes that never have to be washed, because they never get dirty.

Sneaky Shoe Thinks 4U

Runners got a brain-boost in 2005 when a "thinking" sneaker sprinted onto the world scene. The brainy shoe has an in-shoe computer tucked in its arch and magnetic sensors in its heel. Each time a runner's heel strikes the ground, the sensors track changes in weight, pace, and running surface and feed this data to the computer. Then the computer adjusts the shoe's shape and cushioning to suit the speed and power of the stride and terrain underfoot. How's that for making running a no-brainer?

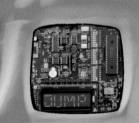

Invisibility Cloak

Ever wished you had an invisibility cloak like Harry Potter? When the hero of J.K. Rowling's blockbuster books wants to get around on the sly, he slips on a magic cloak that makes him invisible to the human eye. Someday, you may be able to do the same. Recently, researchers invented a cloak that makes people appear invisible using science, not magic. The cloak camouflages the wearer to blend in with the background. Made of special material that reflects light, the cloak projects an image of the background behind the wearer onto itself. That way the wearer appears transparent—as if you can see right through him. But the cloak is still visible. So researchers still have work to do if they ever hope to match the magic of fiction.

Handbag Lets Out an Earful

"Listen up, human! This is your handbag talking! You are about to forget your wallet…your keys…your umbrella…." Thanks to recent research such a handbag may not be as far-fetched as it sounds. Researchers have developed computerized fabric patches that you can Velcro together to make a bag that'll tell you if you've forgotten something even before you leave home. The patches contain different parts of this "talking memory system," such as a microcomputer, sensor, radio antenna, receiver, reader, and voice synthesizer. So when you pick up the bag, for example, a sensor in the handle triggers the reader to look for objects the microcomputer is programmed to detect. The radio antenna and receiver then listen for signals from ID tags on your wallet and the like. And if they don't hear the signals, the voice synthesizer lets you know in short order. You might say it delivers a handy earful!

I Want My TMW!

Where can I get a pet TMW? That was the question dozens of people put to *The Orlando Sentinel* on April 1, 1984, when the newspaper ran a story about the TMW—Tasmanian Mock Walrus. The story showed a photo of a 10 cm (4 in.) long rodent whose long front teeth made it look like a mini walrus.

The nearly hairless creature was anything but cute and cuddly. Some people even thought it was downright ugly. Nevertheless, the story reported, hordes of people in Florida were adopting the TMW as a pet.

Please adopt me.

It had the personality of a hamster and purred like a cat. It never needed a bath, used a litter box, and devoured cockroaches for dinner.

According to the story, one TMW was all anyone needed to clean up a house infested with cockroaches. So a local couple was trying to import the unusual creature from Tasmania, Australia, to help fight Florida's exploding roach population. But in the end, everyone desperately seeking a TMW was disappointed. The story was nothing but an April Fools' joke, and the creature shown in the photo was actually a naked mole rat.

When human beings "follow the herd" by thinking and acting just like the group, or general population, some people call them "sheeple."

CHAPTER 4

Humans vs. Animals

It's no secret we Earthlings think we're something special. We've dubbed ourselves "wise man" in Latin (*Homo sapiens)*. And we like to think we're different than the average Tom, Dick, or Hairy animal.

But we human beings need clean air, food, and shelter to survive just like any other animal. Also, research reveals that animals can do many of the things we often think of as "what makes us human," such as using tools and painting pictures. And sometimes animals seem to have a sixth sense all their own. Hunker down with this *Planet Earth News* exclusive to find out how dogs are psychic, birds fish with bait, and monkeys get hooked on video games.

Check out the competition!

Animals Did What?!

Only a human can use tools, play games, and create art, right? Wrong! Check out how animals can do some of the very things we think make us human.

Elephant Gives Picasso Competition

Ruby, the late elephant who lived at the Phoenix Zoo in Arizona, loved to doodle in the sand with her trunk. One day in the 1980s, her zookeeper gave her a stick and encouraged her to draw with it instead. Ruby soon learned how to hold a paintbrush in her trunk and got all charged up about painting with color on canvas. As she painted, Ruby often chose colors that seemed to match new objects in her environment, such as fire trucks or visitors' clothes. Visitors were shocked and amazed as they watched the 2,720 kg (6,000 lb.) pachyderm paint at an easel. Ruby and her paintings became world-famous. In the late 1980s, one of her paintings sold for $5,000!

Birdbrain Goes Fishing with Bait

Fishing rods are for the birds, er, humans. The only tool the green heron needs to catch fish is bait. The resourceful wading bird found in North America, South America, and Japan drops its lure— like a piece of bread—on the water then waits patiently nearby. If the bread floats away, the green heron just picks it up and puts it back in the same spot. And once an unsuspecting fish approaches for a nibble, the brainy bird seizes the fish. Gotcha! What's more, the "fisherbird" can lure fish with almost any kind of bait— worms, flies, twigs, moss, Styrofoam, feathers. A green heron in Florida even caught fish with dog food!

Sea Otter Makes

Sea otters are agile swimmers who spend their whole lives at sea along the west coast of North America. Hanging out in the water 24/7 requires lots of body heat. So sea otters have to eat piles of food to stay warm. Fortunately, the ocean floor is like a seafood buffet for the furry swimmers. Whenever sea otters get hungry, they dive down and pick up prey for a satisfying meal—sea urchins, mussels, crabs, scallops,

EXPOSED!

The bearded vulture, which eats almost nothing but bones, is like a sword-swallowing stunt-person. It drops bones onto rocks to split them apart then swallows the bone slivers whole!

Rats Have the Last Laugh

When researchers tickled rats, the rodents chirped just like they do when they play with each other. The researchers said the rats were laughing. Other scientists disagreed and said "the joke" was on the researchers. Ha, ha!

mashing Meal

abalone, or clams. Then they pack their purchases into "take-out bags," loose pouches of skin in their armpits. Once the otters surface, they float on their backs and use their bellies as a dinner table. The floating diners put a rock on their bellies and smash any mussels or clams against it to crack open the hard shells. What's more, sea otters will stash a favorite rock in their armpit pouches for safekeeping over several dives. Now that's a handy tool!

Monkeys Play Mind Games

The rhesus monkeys learned how to play a video game for a science experiment and got hooked. The game tested memory. It presented a group of pictures followed by a lone picture. Abel and Baker then had to decide if the lone picture had been in the group of pictures by moving the joystick to options for "there," "not there," or "don't know." When humans do memory tests like this, they usually choose "there" for the first and last pictures and "don't know" for those in-between, which we find harder to recall. Believe it or not, the monkeys did the very same thing. Scientists say this shows that monkeys know when they don't know something. The scientists believe this means monkeys can think about thinking, a trait once thought to be only human. Who knew monkeys could play such mind games!

Animal Smarts

Homo sapiens—a.k.a. the wise guys 'n' gals—aren't the only sign of intelligent life on Earth. Far from it! Check out some other animals' smart moves and know-how.

Ants Grow Crops with
Green Thumbs

The leafcutter ants of Central and South America don't need to raid anyone's picnic. They've been growing their own food on farms for 50 million years. That's millions of years before the ancestors of modern-day humans began walking upright, let alone farming crops. Leafcutter ants work together to grow edible fungus in large underground gardens. The six-legged farmers fertilize the crops with leaves and other organic material they collect. What's more, a recent study reveals that leafcutter ants protect their crops from noxious weeds with a natural weed killer. Tiny bacteria, or microorganisms, make the weed killer, and the ants cultivate the microorganisms on a patch of the shell that covers their bodies. How's that for a green thumb, er, shell?

The African grey parrot Alex is a birdbrain like no other. Even though Alex has a brain the size of a walnut, he can talk, count, and identify colors. Dr. Irene Pepperberg began training and studying Alex in 1977. Since then, Alex has learned to name 50 or more objects, such as paper, wood, cork, nuts, grapes, bananas, and water, and tell how many objects up to six are in a group. And the chatty parrot is more than just a talented mimic. He's a tough ol' bird who says what he means and means what he says. For example, Alex loves showers and when he wants one, he'll say, "I want shower." He uses other simple phrases, such as "I want nut" and "Come here." He also knows the word "No" and doesn't hesitate to use it. If a trainer brings him something other than what he asks for, for example, he says "No" then repeats what he wants. One day Pepperberg hopes Alex may even be able to read. Maybe we should call him "Albird Einstein."

Dogs Are Psychic

Nobody knows when children with epilepsy will have a seizure, losing awareness of their surroundings and sometimes control of their limbs. Except for some dogs, that is. A recent study shows that as many as 15 percent of dogs can predict epileptic seizures before they strike. During the study, the dogs gave warning a few minutes before a seizure by licking the child's face, barking, whimpering, or staying by the child's side. Some dogs even seemed to try to protect children from falling by sitting on the children or pushing them away from stairs. Scientists don't know how the dogs know an attack is coming on. Some think the dogs may detect visual signs, such as a change in facial expression, or a change in smell. Now if only dogs could teach ol' humans a new trick!

BEARS GIVE HUNTERS THE SLIP

Hunters beware! Sometimes grizzlies and black bears outwit human hunters by walking backward in their own tracks or trudging over rocks or water to leave no tracks at all.

Is this claim...

A) un-bear-able baloney?
B) an example of animal ingenuity?
C) nothing but a bear-faced joke?
D) based on real-life experiences of bear hunters?

Answers on page 63.

EXPOSED!

One time after keepers at the Oklahoma Zoo washed the floor of an orangutan's cage, the ape ran towards a wet spot and slid across it on both feet. Eyewitnesses say the orangutan looked just like a kid on a skateboard!

Jackalopes Sing the Cowboy Blues

egend has it that jackalopes—jackrabbits with the horns of an antelope, deer or goat—hopped down the trails of the American wild west. Cowboys said the horned critters could use their antlers to fight and their voices to sound like humans.

When cowboys sang around the campfire, the jackalopes supposedly imitated their voices to sing back. What's more, if the cowboys tried to hunt the creatures down, the rabbits mimicked their voices to confuse them. The furry tricksters called out

"Home on the range..."

something like "There he goes, over there," then hopped to it to getaway.

Hundreds of years ago, people also reported jackalope sightings in Europe, and drew pictures of horned rabbits in nature books. Nevertheless, no jackalope has ever been captured alive. Today, scientists think the horned rabbits may have been real, because they've discovered an infectious disease that makes bunnies grow horns. However, the horns are smaller than antlers and infected rabbits can't talk like people. So jackalopes that sing the cowboy blues remain the stuff of legend.

The town of Douglas, Wyoming, celebrates Jackalope Day in June every year. On June 31, people can buy licenses to hunt the legendary creatures from midnight to two A.M.

CHAPTER 5

Look Who's Talking

Y ackety-yak yak yak! No creature can talk your ear off quite like *Homo sapiens*. Our ability to speak and understand each other as we chat, joke around, tell stories, and relay messages and information sets us apart from our closest living relatives—the apes. In fact, some scientists call humans the talking ape!

Today, people speak about 6,000 different languages around the world. When we meet at the United Nations, say, we translate words from one language to another, so people who speak different languages can understand each other. We humans have also invented writing to record our history. Check out this *Planet Earth News* exclusive for the "write" stuff and some riddles carved in stone.

Chatter away!

Speak Up!

Hey, kid! Are you ready to talk the talk? Check out how communication rocks the world.

And the Walls Talk Back

Climbing the walls in a waiting room? Nowadays, if you chat up the walls, they just might talk back. In 2003, a cell phone company in Portugal built a wall of video screens in its waiting room that displays news headlines, short animations, and games. The wall asks people to dial a number on their cell phones and then play the games on its display. Another video wall stands tall in a British TV newsroom, visible from the street through windows. During live interviews, the wall asks passersby to use their cell phones to text message questions for the person being interviewed. Then the wall displays the questions for the person to answer. Just call the wall to have a ball, er, chat!

Me Tarzan, You Jane...

Were those the first words ever spoken by a human? Maybe not. But nobody knows what they were or when they were spoken, because none of our early ancestors are still around to ask. Scientists think speech evolved as the voice box developed along with the brain (see Upper Hand Swells Earthlings' Heads, page 11). When you speak today, for example, you exhale air from your lungs. The air then travels up your windpipe to your voice box, or larynx, where it strikes vocal cords—folds of skin that vibrate with sound. But just how your brain manages to turn your thoughts into speech is still a mystery. What scientists do know is that spoken words allowed early humans to name objects. And by developing language to describe the world around them, early humans were able to think about the world more effectively and communicate those thoughts to build cultures of common understandings. Who knew gabbing could be so thoughtful?

Humans Have the "Write" Stuff

If you've got the "write" stuff, you can make history. Once humans invented writing, we could record events we witnessed. Writing also allows us to pass knowledge, discoveries, and inventions to future generations of people, so they can build upon them instead of starting from square one. Just call it the ultimate "password!" Some of the earliest known writing dates back more than 5,000 years. Ancient Sumerians, who lived in modern-day Iraq, used seals—symbols engraved on cylinders—to identify personal property. Eventually, they began imprinting the seals on wet clay tablets and this developed into writing. By 3200 B.C., the Sumerians were using a reed (dried stalk of marsh grass) to write wedge-shaped symbols called cuneiforms on tablets to tally up grain or cattle. Archeologists have also found ancient Egyptian writing on clay pots from 3300 B.C. These types of writing gave way to the alphabet, which some say is humans' greatest invention.

EXPOSED!

When a TV went on the blink in Oregon in 2004, its cry for help brought the local sheriff to its side. The malfunctioning box emitted the same signal as that used for international distress calls.

Throw Your Dog a Phone!

Brrring! Brrring! Hello?…What's the word?… Have you heard?… In 1876, Alexander Graham Bell invented the telephone to transmit the sound of people's voices over distance. And suddenly, people were able to talk to each other without having to be in the same place. As if that weren't remarkable enough, in 1973, another human invented the cell phone to let people talk to each other as they roamed around the Earth. And today, cell phones aren't just for talking anymore. You can beam text messages, photos, and video with them. You can also tickle your friends with them through text messages that make your friends' cell phones vibrate. What's more, you can give your dog a bone-shaped camera cell phone that fits on its collar. Then you can call Rover to check up on him through the cell phone's camera. If Rover's misbehaving you can tell him he's a "Bad dog" and, if he barks back, you can hear him. Bow wow!

Riddles in Stone

Check out some ancient riddles carved in stone that continue to baffle Earthlings because their answers are lost in time. If only these walls and monuments could talk.

Earthlings Totally Stonewalled

What is the ancient circle of stones on Salisbury Plain in Wiltshire, England? Is it a circle of giant doorways to another world? A corral for cows? A UFO landing pad? Nothing fires up people's imaginations quite like Stonehenge. What spurred Stone Age humans to build the strange circle? In the 1960s, a scientist used a computer to check the stones' positions against movements of the Sun and Moon. He concluded that Stonehenge is an ancient "computer" for predicting Moon eclipses! Later, research confirmed that the stones align with movements of the Sun, Moon, and stars. Even so, no one can say the stones were used that way for sure. So the mystery of Stonehenge continues to stonewall us!

Stoneheads Go for Stroll

Easter Island in the South Pacific is the most remote, inhabited place on Earth—and one of the most eerie. Stone statues of massive human heads stand along the coast with their backs to the sea. The average statue is almost twice as tall as a pro basketball player and weighs as much as seven blue whales. Ancient islanders carved the giant heads and just how they moved the statues from stone quarries to the coast is still a mystery. Local legend has it that the stoneheads walked out of the quarries to their coastal lookouts. But scientists think the islanders strapped the stoneheads onto wooden sleds then rolled the sleds over logs. Experiments show that the wooden-sled theory works. Still, we may never know if that's how the ancient islanders really did it. All we can say for sure is that stoneheads will roll!

EXPOSED!

Ancient Egyptian wall paintings tell us that the Egyptians knew how to have a ball. The walls show pictures of people playing Monkey in the Middle.

ALIEN SPACESHIP LANDING STRIP?

Peer down from an airplane above Nazca, Peru, and you'll see perfectly straight lines several kilometres long drawn on the desert ground. An archeologist discovered the lines in 1926 and since then some people have thought the lines are an extraterrestrial landing strip visible only from the air.

Were the lines...

A) a quirk of nature?
B) a human-made geometry exercise?
C) runways drawn by alien visitors?
D) drawn by ancient Peruvians?

Answers on page 63.

The Sphinx Stumps Earthlings

Everybody knows that the stone statue of the Sphinx at Giza, Egypt, cannot utter a single word. But the Sphinx bedevils Earthlings with riddles nevertheless. As people lay eyes on the towering statue of a man's head with a lion's body, they often wonder who carved the strange figure out of a mound of rock, and why? Did the ancient carvers build it to guard the pyramids nearby? What did a lion with a human head represent back then? And just how old is the Sphinx anyway? Much to many Earthlings' chagrin, nobody can really say for sure. Archeologists think that the Sphinx was built in 2500 B.C. by Khafre, an ancient Egyptian pharaoh who constructed some of the neighboring pyramids. But some geologists, scientists who study the Earth's history through rocks, disagree. They say erosion, or wearing down of the statue by wind and rain, shows that the Sphinx was built thousands of years earlier. And the Sphinx? Well, the stone-faced riddler just keeps smiling without giving anything away.

PLANET EARTH NEWS

presents **Tales That Got Us**

Lost City of Atlantis
Found—Again!

Ever since Plato, an ancient Greek thinker, wrote about Atlantis about 2,400 years ago, people have debated its existence and searched the Earth for the fantastic island. According to Plato, the island city lay in the Atlantic Ocean around 10,000 B.C., thousands of years before any ancient city we know of existed.

Plato described Atlantis as a sunny paradise where elephants roamed, luscious fruit grew, and people lived in palaces of silver and gold. He wrote that the Atlanteans built an army to take over the world. Then

Something's fishy.

one day an earthquake sunk the island; Atlantis vanished beneath the sea.

Plato's student Aristotle, a famous thinker himself, said Plato had made up the whole story to make the point that great wealth and power can corrupt people. But other thinkers said the story was pure fact, and so goes the debate to this day. What's more, over the years, people have claimed to have discovered Atlantis. Nevertheless, no solid proof has ever turned up, and Plato's tale has yet to become all washed-up!

In the 1500s, after Europeans had discovered North and South America, mapmakers often labeled the continents Atlantis. If the name had stuck, you'd be living in Atlantis!

CHAPTER 6

The Ultimate Copycats

Earthlings are cool cats. What other creature has invented Ghost Away spray (see page 50) to fend off make-believe monsters and spring-loaded sneakers to run with boing (see page 25)? But did you know that Earthlings are also the biggest copycats on the planet?

The shocking truth is that *Homo sapiens* often copy nature's designs outright when we invent things. When the Wright brothers invented the airplane, for example, they studied vultures to learn how the birds' wings gave them lift. And copying nature like this is nothing for Earthlings to be ashamed of. It's a smart move. Check out this *Planet Earth News* exclusive to see how plants and animals have inspired Earthlings to turn miners into human worms, copy burrs to stick it to the world, and try to unlock nature's secrets of survival for superhuman powers.

What's up, copycat?

Wild Ideas

Wow! Look at that worm, dog, or lobster go! Discover how the remarkable know-how of nature has inspired humans to create truly wild structures and machines.

Engineer Turns Miners into Human Worms

Build a tunnel under England's Thames River? "Impossible," declared engineers in 1818, after many failed attempts. Water and mud always seeped down from above, collapsing the tunnel in a soggy heap. But one innovative engineer solved the problem by turning miners into "tunneling machines," like the shipworm *Teredo* *navalis*. The shipworm easily bores through ships' wooden hulls using a hard shell on its head to support its boring hole. The engineer designed a similar box-shaped shield that supported the ground overhead, allowing miners to dig through and secure the tunnel with brick. And humans still build tunnels this way today.

Eiffel Tower has Human Legs

The Eiffel Tower in Paris, France, has not one but four legs to stand on. And those legs aren't just any old legs, they're giant replicas of the human thighbone. When Gustave Eiffel built the famous tower for the 1889 World's Fair, the thigh-bone's design inspired him. Eiffel made the tower's legs in the same shape and patterned an iron lattice of braces inside the legs after the ridges in the bone. Once he was done, the 300 m (984 ft.) tower was the tallest building in the world, and it remained so until the Chrysler building was built in 1930.

Sticky Icky Burrs Spur Inventor

Burrs have covered my pants and they won't let go! In the 1940's, when Swiss inventor George de Mestral had a tough time removing a plant's prickly burrs from his pants, he looked at them under a microscope to find out why. De Mestral discovered tiny hooks on the burrs that latched onto loops in the fabric of this pants. He thought that these hooks and loops would make a great fastener for sticking materials together. So he took this design and stuck it on the world, inventing Velcro.

Sailor Goes to the Dogs for Sole

Slip sliding away! That's what Paul Sperry found himself doing on the wet decks of his sailboat in 1935. The avid sailor wanted a pair of shoes that wouldn't skid on the wet surface. But none did the trick. Then one winter day while he was walking his dog, Sperry noticed that the cocker spaniel wasn't slipping all over the icy streets like he was. What was the dog's sure-footed secret? Sperry looked closely at the dog's paw and discovered wavelike grooves on its sole. Then he took a razor blade, copied the wavelike pattern into rubber, attached the rubber to a pair of canvas sneakers, and laced them up. With that the first pair of non-skid deck shoes trotted into the world. Now that's something to bark home about!

FICTION VS REALITY

Wing it Like a Bird, Dude!

People have wanted to fly like birds for eons. In a Greek myth, Icarus escapes the island of Crete by flying on artificial wings made of feathers and wax. But when the winged flyboy flies close to the sun, the wax melts and he falls into the sea. What's more, the first flying machines people built had flapping devices that attached to the human body like bird wings. However, all these flying machines failed. People just don't have the design of muscle and bone that allows birds to fly. But in 1977, an aircraft powered by human muscle finally soared. Aeronautics engineer Paul MacCready built the *Gossamer Condor*, a one-seater that flew on a pilot's pedal power.

Robo-Lobster
Hunts Mines for Breakfast

Not many creatures can get around the ocean floor like the lob-ster. A live lobster can walk in any direction—forward, back-ward, or side-to-side—switch direction step-by-step, and crawl over and around rocks or seaweed with ease. It runs through these maneuvers all in a day's hunt for food. So when scientists wanted to build a robot to search for mines in the ocean, the lobster seemed like the perfect model. The scientists studied how the eight-legged, shelled creature moves, how its muscles and nerves work, and how its antennae sense objects. Then they built Robo-Lobster, a 3 kg (7 lb.) plastic robot whose body shape, movements, and antennae mimic a live lobster as it scurries through the ocean hunt-ing down explosive mines for breakfast.

EXPOSED!

What's one creature Earthlings don't want to copy? Dinosaurs! Humans don't want to become extinct. No wonder we're trying to figure out what killed off the dinosaurs!

Nobody Does It Better

When it comes to walking on ceilings or regrowing a leg, nobody does it better than animals. Check out some of their remarkable abilities that scientists are trying to copy for superhuman powers.

USED SHELLS

Seashell Shield
Stops Scientists Cold

What's made of chalk but is tough enough to survive being run over by a truck without cracking? The helmetlike shell of an abalone snail. According to scientists, the mother-of-pearl lined seashell, which protects the snail from predators, is one of the toughest materials on Earth. How can something made of brittle chalk be so strong? Scientists think the shell's strength comes from its structure. Under a microscope, the shell reveals layers of "tiles" stuck together by a gluey protein. This glue has the strength to hold the layers together and the flexibility to allow the layers to slide apart, absorbing the impact of a heavy blow without breaking. Now scientists are copying the shell's layered structure to try to make lightweight body armor that'll stop bullets cold.

Gecko-Girl
Walks on Ceiling

Move over, Spider-Man! Once Gecko-Girl puts on her special climbing gear, she may be able to walk upside down on ceilings, climb walls, and scale cliffs lickety-split just like the sticky-footed lizard whose name she bears. Just how do the little lizards do it? Scientists came up with lots of theories, but the mystery remained unsolved until they studied the millions of tiny hairs that cover geckos' feet. As a gecko takes a step, its foot and toes drag the hairs forward, which makes the hairs stick to the climbing surface. Then, as it takes another step, it peels its foot off the surface just like you peel off Scotch tape. Now, scientists are trying to copy this sticking power to make "gecko tape" that astronauts could use to attach equipment outside the space station. And one day they hope to make climbing gear that could turn the girl next door into Gecko-Girl.

Space—Astronauts Just Can't **Bear** It

Floating in space may sound like fun, but astronauts can't bear it for long. Studies show that astronauts lose bone mass during long spaceflights. Scientists think the weightlessness they experience as they no longer feel the pull of Earth's gravity is the thieving culprit. But if astronauts could hibernate like bears, they might be able to grin and bear it for long missions to far-away planets. No joke! When bears hibernate, or sleep through winter, their bones experience less stress like those of astronauts in space. But unlike astronauts, bears don't lose much bone mass or muscle tone. So some scientists are boning up on hibernation to see if astronauts might be able to hibernate through long space missions one day.

EXPOSED!

Meow! A man who thought he was a cat began mewing for help when he got stuck up a tree. Local kids failed to coax him down with a saucer of milk, so the fire department rescued him.

Hoax Busters!

MUTANT WORMS FIND FOUNTAIN OF YOUTH

Roundworms—tiny worms about a millimetre long—have altered genes that allow them to live twice as long as their wormy relatives. One day scientists hope to bottle the mutants' anti-aging secret into pills that people can take to live longer.

Are the long-lived wrigglers...

A) good at hiding wrinkles?
B) a spineless hoax?
C) a squirmy quirk of nature?
D) a bona fide bottling clue to the fountain of youth?

Answers on page 63.

Newt Kid on the Block Goes Out on a Limb

Say, just say, you lost a leg and three months later you had managed to regrow it. Chances are people would call you a boy wonder, but those in the know might call you the "newt kid on the block." Huh? Unlike people, newts can regrow legs, arms, tails, and even parts of their hearts and eyes at the drop of a hat, er, limb. When the small lizardlike creatures lose a leg, for example, they can grow a new leg that has the same size and function of the old one in just a few months. In fact, some scientists are studying the amazing regenerating ability of newts to figure out how they do it and if modern medicine could use their techniques with humans. But other scientists think it'll never happen. So you might say the newt researchers are going out on a limb!

Miracle **Roach** Pills
Cure All Ills

Got a nasty cold, the world's worst case of acne, or any other illness known to humans? Take two of Dr. Gregor's cockroach pills and you'll be cured. Sound far-fetched? On May 21, 1981, Dr. Gregor, an entomologist, or scientist who studies insects, announced that he had made pills that fit that very bill.

Dr. Gregor told the press he had bred a variety of super-roaches that were resistant to poison and radiation and had turned their juice into pills. He claimed the roach pills had cured people from lots of ills and brought out 70

Super Roach to the rescue.

patients to back him up. And people believed him. Maybe that's because the remarkable survival powers of roaches, such as the ability to live headless for a week, were so well-known. Over 175 newspapers ran stories about the miraculous bug drug.

Later, Dr. Gregor confessed it was all a hoax. The entomologist revealed his true identity: Joey Skaggs, journalism teacher. Skaggs believed the press was incredibly gullible and had set out to prove it to his students. So as it turned out, Dr. Gregor was a real pill after all!

Cockroaches have superhuman survival power. Unlike people, roaches can survive direct exposure to a nuclear explosion.

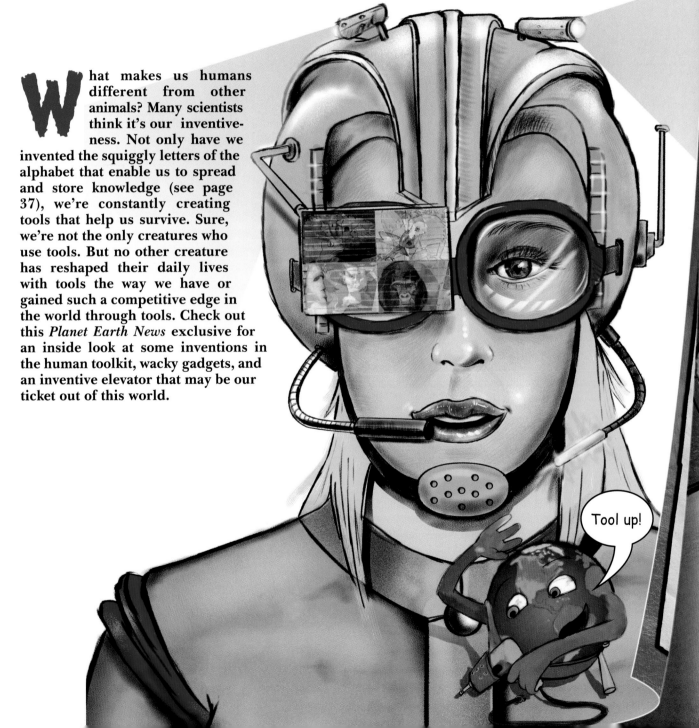

CHAPTER 7

Creatures of Invention

What makes us humans different from other animals? Many scientists think it's our inventiveness. Not only have we invented the squiggly letters of the alphabet that enable us to spread and store knowledge (see page 37), we're constantly creating tools that help us survive. Sure, we're not the only creatures who use tools. But no other creature has reshaped their daily lives with tools the way we have or gained such a competitive edge in the world through tools. Check out this *Planet Earth News* exclusive for an inside look at some inventions in the human toolkit, wacky gadgets, and an inventive elevator that may be our ticket out of this world.

Tool up!

School of Cool Tools

Wanna rock your world? Check out the "school of cool tools" where humans learned to make fire with stones and invent devices that changed our lives.

Computers
Take Over the World

Once upon a time, people were computers. The word "computer" meant a person who did computations, or calculations, for there were no computers as we know them today. People didn't build the first fully electronic computer until 1945. The house-sized device whizzed through 5,000 functions per second.

Today, supercomputers can perform about 280 trillion operations per second and, unlike people, they do it flawlessly. We've programmed computers to forecast weather, control cars and factories, and scan groceries. This frees up our brains to think about life, the universe, and everything else. So computers just may give us more brain power.

Pop Goes the Wheel-ie

Whether you pop 'em, spin 'em, or roll 'em, wheels rule. Nothing people have invented has made working and getting around the world as easy as the wheel. Archeologists think people in Mesopotamia—modern-day Iraq—invented the first wheel as a turntable to make pottery around 3500 B.C.

An image dated back to 3200 B. shows a cart with solid wheels, which may have been the first kind vehicle people put on wheels. Ancie Egyptian wall paintings show spoke-wheeled chariots. Eventually, people als invented toothed wheels, like bike gears, to run machines; grooved wheels to operate weight-bearing pulleys and cranes; and fly-wheels to power up engines. We also got ou own wheels, inventing bicycles, cars, scoote inline skates, and skateboards that help us around much farther and faster than we ca on our own two legs.

Everybody Was Struck by Lightning

Boom! Cra-a-ack! Sizzle! A bolt of lightning shot down from the sky, set a tree ablaze, and lit up our ancestors' world. Chances are that was the scene when early humans discovered fire. Evidence suggests they used fire 1 million years ago. But not all scientists agree. One thing's for sure: those flames got our ancestors all fired up. Fire was the first energy source people found beyond the human body. Early humans learned how to keep its flames alive and use fire as a tool. They huddled around fire for warmth, lit torches to see in the dark, set blazes to keep wild beasts away, and barbecued woolly mammoths for dinner. The portable heat source also allowed humans to move to areas with cooler climates and make tools like they never had before. Eventually, people fired up pottery, cooked grains, and learned how to make fire by rubbing sticks or stones. Today, we burn fossil fuels to run machines that do much more work than we ever could on our own steam. How's that for a stroke of genius, er, lightning?

Computer
Is a No-Brainer!

Sure, computers beat people at math, but no computer is capable of human intelligence. That's because we don't fully understand how the brain works. Scientists are trying to reveal the brain's mysteries by building a computer model of it. Go figure!

EXPOSED!

Inventing the airplane gave humans the means to travel far and wide faster than ever before. While the average person can walk about 6 km/h (4 mph), some airplanes can carry people 2,150 km/h (1,336 mph)!

Wacky Gadgets

Not many a human can resist a cool gadget, that does something unexpected or funny. Just check out some incredible gadgets people have invented.

Spray Keeps Monsters Away

Poof! Make-believe monsters that hide under the bed are all in your head. But that hasn't stopped Mary Feldman of Charleston, South Carolina, from inventing Ghost Away— a spray to keep those imaginary monsters at bay.

In fact, the play spray is made of chamomile, white and yellow daisy-like flowers that would not harm a hair on any creature's head. How's that for spooky, er, spoofy action?

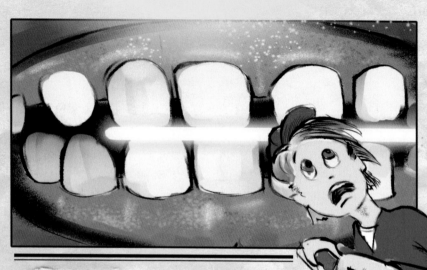

Lightsabers
Defend Your Gums

Put your lightsaber where your mouth is, kiddo! In the future, that may be the advice your dentist gives you to win the battle against disease-causing bacteria that like to hunker down and multiply between your teeth and gums. Even though the toothbrush has come a long way since early humans cleaned their teeth with grass stalks and tree twigs, researchers hope to improve upon it still. They've invented a mini lightsaber, or handheld blue light, that kills "bad" bacteria by shining on it and leaves "good" bacteria unharmed. In fact, the researchers say that shining the lightsaber on your teeth and gums for two minutes a day may even prevent, treat, or control gum disease. May the force be with you!

Pogo Has Mojo

What do you get when a world champion skateboarder who likes big air and a scientist who designs rubberlike springs put their heads together? A pogo stick with mojo! Skateboarder Andy Macdonald and scientist Bruce Middleton recently designed the Flybar, an aluminum pogo stick that can propel riders three or four times higher than the average pogo stick. Instead of bouncing on a metal spring, the Flybar bounces on 12 large rubber bands like a trampoline. As a rider's feet press down on the footholds, the rubber bands stretch down. Then they snap back up— thrusting the rider into the air. Boing!

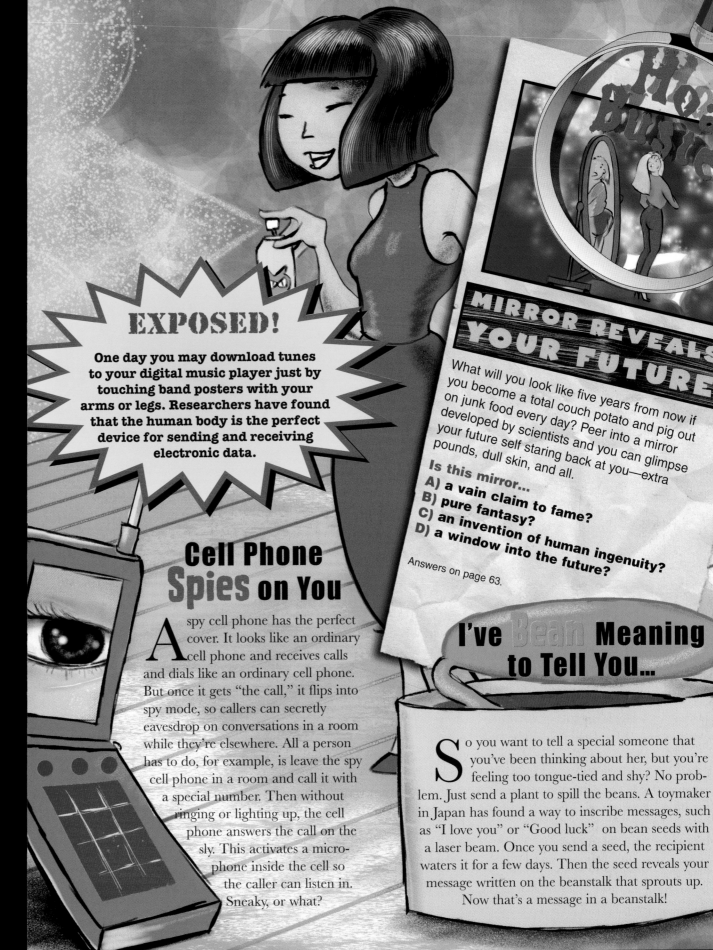

EXPOSED!

One day you may download tunes to your digital music player just by touching band posters with your arms or legs. Researchers have found that the human body is the perfect device for sending and receiving electronic data.

Cell Phone Spies on You

A spy cell phone has the perfect cover. It looks like an ordinary cell phone and receives calls and dials like an ordinary cell phone. But once it gets "the call," it flips into spy mode, so callers can secretly eavesdrop on conversations in a room while they're elsewhere. All a person has to do, for example, is leave the spy cell phone in a room and call it with a special number. Then without ringing or lighting up, the cell phone answers the call on the sly. This activates a microphone inside the cell so the caller can listen in. Sneaky, or what?

MIRROR REVEALS YOUR FUTURE

What will you look like five years from now if you become a total couch potato and pig out on junk food every day? Peer into a mirror developed by scientists and you can glimpse your future self staring back at you—extra pounds, dull skin, and all.

Is this mirror...
A) a vain claim to fame?
B) pure fantasy?
C) an invention of human ingenuity?
D) a window into the future?

Answers on page 63.

I've Bean Meaning to Tell You...

So you want to tell a special someone that you've been thinking about her, but you're feeling too tongue-tied and shy? No problem. Just send a plant to spill the beans. A toymaker in Japan has found a way to inscribe messages, such as "I love you" or "Good luck" on bean seeds with a laser beam. Once you send a seed, the recipient waters it for a few days. Then the seed reveals your message written on the beanstalk that sprouts up. Now that's a message in a beanstalk!

The Idea Lab

Take a sneak peek at some fabulous devices in the works that may one day allow humans to go where and how no human has ever gone before.

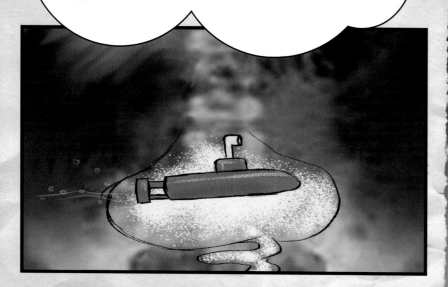

Tiny Sub Dives Inside...YOU!

Believe it or not, scientists recently built a tiny submarine to cruise through blood vessels in the human body. The 4 mm (¹/₈ in.) long sub doesn't carry shrunken doctors though. But doctors can drive it via remote control and TV screens that show its whereabouts. The medical sub carries sensors onboard for checking body functions. It can also carry cargo such as medicine for special delivery to infected areas. Researchers are still working out the details of "inner body travel" to make the sub "human-worthy." One day, they hope the tiny sub may be able to detect and repair damaged body tissues and "torpedo" cancer cells. Pow!

Elevator to Space

Going up! Next floor: Outer space! In 1979, Arthur C. Clarke wrote about a space elevator in his science-fiction novel *Fountains of Paradise*. Clarke's elevator traveled along a cable made of material that was thinner than dental floss but much stronger than steel. Well, at the time, no such material existed. But in 1991, a scientist discovered carbon nanotubes—microscopic sheets of carbon rolled into tubes that are hundreds of times stronger than steel. If these tubes could be strung together, a carbon-nanotube cable as thin as sewing thread could hoist a large car. So some scientists think that if the tiny carbon tubes could be linked into a 13–25 cm (5–10 in.) wide ribbon, the material would be strong enough to support a real space elevator. Design and construction details are underway. Stay tuned for a lift!

Make Your Own
Body Double

Ever wish you could be in two places at once? Someday "claytronics"—tiny robots that can stick together like clay and turn into any 3-D object—may be able to make that wish come true. Say you have a soccer game at the same time as a doctor's appointment, for example. If scientists succeed in developing claytronics as they hope, you could go to the game and send video images of yourself via the Internet to your doctor. And as long as your doctor had a lump of "claytronics" at the office, the tiny robots could receive the images of you then shape-shift to replicate your body for the checkup. Then, if you had a lump of the stuff and a wireless Internet connection at the soccer game, the doctor could send a copy of herself to you to check your reflexes as she sat in front of a video camera at her office tapping the knee of your digital body double. Presto!

Beam Me up, Scotty!

Traveling took no time at all in the original *Star Trek* TV show. Captain Kirk just went to the "transporter room." Then engineer Scotty dematerialized his body into glittery bits and beamed them down to another planet where Kirk rematerialized instantly. And once Kirk was ready to return he'd just say, "Beam me up, Scotty!" Today, scientists are researching instant travel, or teleportation, like this. But they don't expect it to become a reality for humans any time soon—if ever. The scientists are working with atoms, the microscopic building blocks that make up all matter in the universe. In order to teleport a person, scientists would have to build a machine capable of precisely locating, tracking, and reassembling the trillions and trillions of atoms that make up the human body. If even a few atoms were reassembled slightly askew, a traveler might end up physically or mentally damaged on arrival. And we humans prefer to arrive completely intact. Let the research continue.

Machine Turns Soil into Cereal

Extra! Extra! The Wizard of Menlo Park has invented a food machine that can turn soil into cereal and water into wine! That was the story *The Daily Graphic* ran on April 1, 1878. The newspaper announced that the famous inventor Thomas Edison, who founded an "invention factory" in Menlo Park, New Jersey, had built a machine that could end world hunger by transforming ordinary elements into food.

Several other newspapers then rushed to hail Edison's remarkable achievement with stories of their own.

A serial inventor strikes.

After that, *The Daily Graphic* revealed that the story was an April Fools' joke, reprinting another newspaper's article under the headline "They Bite!"

The other papers probably bit *The Daily Graphic*'s bait, because Thomas Edison had already pulled many ground-breaking devices out of his inventor's hat. Just the year before, Edison had invented the phonograph, one of the earliest machines that could record and play sound. And later he invented the electric light bulb that eventually lit homes, buildings, and streets all over the planet.

Thomas Edison is the greatest inventor of the modern world. He thought failures in the lab brought him one step closer to success.

CHAPTER 8

Is Anybody Out There?

Are we alone? Is any intelligent life out there somewhere? Not many questions fascinate Earthlings quite like these. Ever since humans have walked the Earth, we've explored far-flung corners of the planet in search of fellow intelligent beings and whatever other interesting creatures we might happen to meet. More recently, we've also set our sights on the skies above, hunting for signs of extraterrestrial life. Maybe that's because the discovery of any such creatures might help us understand more about ourselves. Check out the alien details in this *Planet Earth News* exclusive and find out how we may not be home alone on Earth.

Hunting for Aliens

Earthlings to E. T.: Come out, come out, wherever you are. With 125 billion or so galaxies out there in the universe, it's almost impossible to know where or how to look. But that hasn't stopped Earthlings from trying.

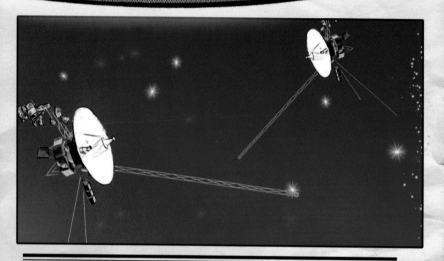

Twins to Greet Aliens

Earthlings launched the *Voyager* spacecraft twins in 1977 with the mission to explore the solar system and beyond—and to deliver a message. People gave the *Voyager* twins a greeting for any civilizations the spacecraft might encounter on their travels. They placed golden disks onboard each spacecraft that contained spoken greetings from Earthlings in 55 languages, music from different cultures and times, and a variety of natural images and sounds, such as wind, thunder, birds, and whales. The idea was to show aliens the life and culture on Earth. Since their launch, *Voyager 1* and *2* have flown by Jupiter, Saturn, Uranus, and Neptune. *Voyager 1* is now the farthest human-made object from the sun. Who knows whom the twins may meet and greet out there?!

Shhh! The Earthlings Are Listening

How do you look for signs of intelligent life in the universe when you can't survive beyond your home planet long enough to travel far and wide through outer space? In 1960, scientist Frank Drake came up with an interesting solution to this problem. Drake realized that he and fellow Earthlings were broadcasting our existence to the rest of the universe via the signals that transmit radio and TV programs. If other intelligent beings could find Earthlings from radio and TV signals, thought Drake, we could find other intelligent beings by listening for their electronic signals. And with that, SETI (Search for Extraterrestrial Intelligence) took off to search the skies for alien signals using radio telescopes. Since then, several SETI projects have sprung up. Today, the average Joe or Jane can even participate from the comfort of his or her own home using a computer to analyze collected data. Nevertheless, Earthlings have yet to find any evidence of extraterrestrials.

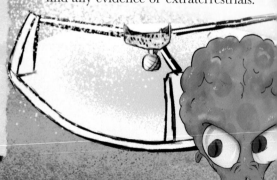

E.T. Phone Earth

It called from outer space. It came from no Earthly source, aircraft, spacecraft, or known nearby star. That's what SETI researcher Jerry Ehman realized when Big Ear, a radio telescope in Delaware, Ohio, picked up an odd signal in 1977. The signal rose high above the daily background noise of the universe for 37 seconds then fell back down into the din and was never heard again. It was the strangest signal Ehman had ever seen. He scribbled "Wow!" on a computer printout of it, and people have called it the Wow! Signal ever since. Many people have tried to decode the signal's letters and numbers in the printout—6EQUJ5—with the hope of deciphering a message from extraterrestrials. But SETI researchers say the letters and numbers stand only for the strength and duration of the signal. Still, many Earthlings just don't seem to get the message....

Hoax Busters

ALIEN INVADES LONDON

On March 31, 1989, thousands of drivers cruising along a highway outside London, England, saw a UFO beaming down upon the city. When the flying saucer landed in a field, a police officer knocked on its door and an alien in a silver suit popped out.

Is this story...

A) an early April Fools' joke?
B) completely bogus?
C) a true tale of a hoax?
D) a true alien sighting?

Answers on page 63.

UFO Crashes the Planet

Flash! Bang! BOOM! Something crashed in the desert near Roswell, New Mexico, in 1947. Rancher W.W. Brazel discovered a strange wreckage of rubber strips, tinfoil, wood sticks, and Scotch tape. Brazel told the local sheriff he might have found a flying disk. The Sheriff told the army, and the army told the press they had captured a flying saucer. The news spread like wildfire. The army's phones rang nonstop with inquiries from news reporters, and Earthlings the world over glued their eyes on the skies. But the very next day, the army retracted the story. They said the wreckage was the remains a high-flying weather balloon, not a flying saucer at all. However, the explanation failed to satisfy everyone, and to this day, some Earthlings believe a UFO crash-landed at Roswell.

EXPOSED!

In 1995, an English businessman declared he had autopsy footage of an alien that died in the Roswell crash. But UFO and special effects experts decided the film was an Earthly hoax.

Next-door Strangers

Y ou don't have to search outer space for interesting company to hang out with. Sometimes, there are some right next-door and you just don't know it until you look.

Hobbits
are For Real

L ong ago, on a remote Indonesian island named Flores, little people lived in caves and hunted dwarf elephants. That was the legend until 2004, when the story turned out to be true. Scientists found the skeleton of an adult woman, who had stood no more than 1 m (3 ft.) tall, buried in a cave on Flores. They also found remains of six other hobbit-sized humans. The "hobbits" lived about 13,000 years ago, when humans like us were out and about the Earth. They walked upright, had a brain the size of a grapefruit, used simple tools, and hunted a now extinct miniature elephant. This discovery of another human species shocked people the world over.

Pongo of the Congo Rules

T he thing was huge. It was hairy all over and it looked like it was half-man, half-beast…. Reports of a monstrous creature the locals called Pongo began trickling out of the Congo, or the heart of Africa, in 1625. That year English explorer Andrew Battel wrote:

This Pongo is in all proportions like a man…he is very tall, and hath a man's face….His bodie is full of haire….

Battel said grown Pongos were so strong that ten men couldn't hold one of them. But most people thought Pongos were pure myth for the next 220 years. It wasn't until 1846 that Dr. Thomas Savage discovered that the Pongo was an unknown ape species. Savage called Pongo the gorilla and today we know that the great ape is one of human beings' closest living relatives.

Tarzan of the Apes Lives!

No, not Tarzan who swings across the movie screen, but the orangutan of Sumatra and Borneo in Indonesia. In the Malayan language, the name *orangutan* means "jungle man." After chimps and gorillas, the orangutan is humans' next closest living relative. What's more, it began swinging from tree to tree Tarzan-style long before the fictional hero was ever created. The orangutan's long arms reach out to grab distant branches with hooklike hands. Unlike other great apes, the orangutan spends most of its life in trees, making it very difficult to find. In fact, an unknown group of orangutans in Borneo remained hidden from Earthlings until 2002.

MERMAID MAKES A SPLASH

In 1842, crowds of New Yorkers flocked to see a wonder of the natural world—the Fejee Mermaid. An English scientist claimed fishermen had caught the unusual half-human, half fish specimen near the "Fejee" Islands of the South Pacific, and that he had picked it up for a natural history museum in London.

Was the mermaid...

A) a creature of nature?
B) a specimen of phony baloney?
C) a monkey with a fish tail?
D) living proof that mermaids exist?

Answers on page 63.

EXPOSED!

Chimpanzees are the closest living relatives of modern-day humans. Almost 99 percent of chimp DNA—proteins that make up their bodies—is exactly the same as human DNA.

10 POINTS

Monsters Afoot

It's a man…it's an ape…it's Bigfoot. No monsters make Earthlings go ape quite like those that look half-ape and half-human. Get the scoop.

Spawn of King Kong?

Is Bigfoot the spawn of King Kong? You can't answer this monster of a question without getting past a dragon first! In 1935, a professor found a fossilized "dragon tooth" that belonged to *Gigantopithecus*, the largest primate that ever lived. It stood 3 m (10 ft.) tall and weighed a mighty 544 kg (1,200 lbs.). Talk about King Kong! Scientists think the huge ape went extinct during an ice age about 500,000 years ago. Today, all that remains of it are teeth and a few jawbones. But scientific models of *Gigantopithecus* look like Bigfoot—the giant hairy creature that witnesses say walks on two legs. Some people think Bigfoot may be a descendant of *Gigantopithecus*. But others think Bigfoot is just a myth. And since no bones or teeth of Bigfoot have ever turned up, the answer to this monster of a question remains at large.

EXPOSED!

Orangutans often wander the forest solo. So some people think the shaggy red-haired Yeren may be an ancient kind of orangutan that still survives.

BIGFOOT WANTED
DEAD OR ALIVE

People around the world report sightings of massive hairy creatures that look and walk like humans. But not one of these big-footed beasts has ever been caught to prove it really exists. Feast your eyes on this gallery of legendary monsters.

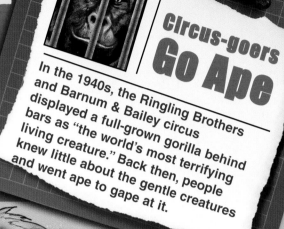
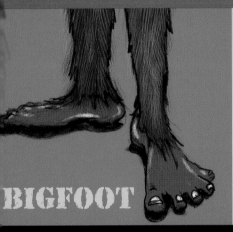

BIGFOOT

Alias: Sasquatch—the Native word for "wild man of the woods"
Spotted: Walking on two legs along the Nelson River in Manitoba, Canada.

YETI

Alias: Abominable Snowman
Spotted: Howling and snarling in the snowfields of the Himalayan mountains of Asia.

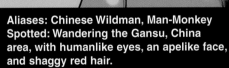

YEREN

Aliases: Chinese Wildman, Man-Monkey
Spotted: Wandering the Gansu, China area, with humanlike eyes, an apelike face, and shaggy red hair.

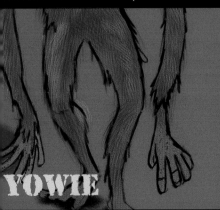

YOWIE

Alias: Bigfoot of the Bush
Spotted: Haunting thick forests in Australia with a loping gait and long arms

ALMA

Alias: Wild Man
Spotted: Lurking in the mountains of Russia and China with a

EL SISIMITE

Alias: Tzitzimitl
Spotted: In the forest of Belize, Central America, with four fingers, no thumbs, and

Bigfoot Caught on Film

Bigfoot's big break.

When Bigfoot hunters Roger Patterson and Bob Gimlin came around a bend at Bluff Creek, California, in 1967, they found what they were looking for: A huge hairy creature standing on two legs.

Patterson grabbed his movie camera and began filming before the creature vanished into the forest. The footage ignited a hot debate. Some scientists said the film was credible evidence of Bigfoot's existence, and that the movements of the monster's muscles couldn't have been faked. Others disagreed. They said the film revealed nothing but a man dressed in a fur suit.

Thirty years later, a Hollywood film director said the real star of the film was an ape suit made by John Chambers, costume designer for the 1967 movie *Planet of the Apes*. But Chambers insisted he had nothing to do with the Bigfoot film. Later in 2004, Bob Heironimus confessed that he was the man who wore the ape suit in the film. But not everyone believed him. Only one thing's for sure: One side or the other—Bigfoot believers or non-believers— is sticking a big foot in its mouth.

In 1930, Rent Mullins faked Bigfoot tracks near a huckleberry patch in Washington State. He had a friend strap on a pair of huge wooden feet and walk around. Just call him Huckleberry Foot!

Answers

Humans Become Computer Networks, page 9

Give yourself five points if you chose D and ten points if you chose C. Believe it or not, the software company Microsoft has patented, or secured the sole right to, the idea to make the human body a computer network. And Microsoft's lab is not the first to experiment with the idea.

Mummies Crack Cold Case, page 19

Give yourself five points if you chose D or ten points if you chose C. This is the true story of the disastrous Franklin Expedition to find a passage to China and India through the frozen waters of the Arctic in the 1840s. In the 1980s, scientists tried to determine exactly how the men had died. They studied the naturally frozen mummies of the men that lay in the Arctic. And from these studies, the mummies indicated that the men had died of lead poisoning. The expedition had set out with the latest and greatest in survival gear, including loads of newfangled tinned food. The tins had been soldered together with lead, which seeped into the food. As the men ate the food, the lead piled up in their bodies, eventually killing them.

Bears Give Hunters the Slip, page 33

Give yourself five points if you chose D or ten points if you chose B. Both grizzlies and black bears have been known to foil human hunters by walking backward in their own tracks or traveling over rocks and water to leave no paw prints. In 1970, a grizzly killed an experienced hunter who was hot on its heels. Investigators think the bear realized the hunter was following it. Here's why: The grizzly circled around a little hill, met up with its own tracks, then snuck up behind the hunter and attacked.

Alien Spaceship Landing Strip?, page 39

Give yourself five points if you chose B or ten points if you chose D. Archeologists think the lines and other drawings scattered over the desert area, such as lizards, monkeys, and whales, were drawn by the Nazca who lived in Peru about a thousand years ago. But how the ancient people drew the lines so straight and the figures so big and what exactly they used them for remain a mystery. Some archeologists think the straight lines may have been pathways or connections to water.

Mutant Worms Find Fountain of Youth, page 45

Give yourself five points if you chose C or ten points if you chose D. The long-lived wrigglers are a quirk of nature that scientists discovered in the 1980s, and one day they may help scientists bottle a fountain of youth for people. All living beings inherit genes from their parents that determine characteristics, such as hair and eye color. What's more, worms have all the types of cells that people do. Scientists have discovered that certain genes in the worms control aging, and that by turning these genes "off" they can increase the worms' life span to six times that of the average roundworm. Now scientists are trying to develop pills that can copy these effects on people's genes.

Mirror Reveals Your Future, page 51

Give yourself five points if you chose D or ten points if you chose C. Researchers in France have developed a mirror that reflects what your future self will look like. Wireless cameras set up around your house photograph you to help a computer build a profile of your lifestyle. Then image-processing technology helps the mirror conjure up a picture of how that lifestyle will shape your body and color your cheeks.

Alien Invades London, page 57

Give yourself five points if you chose C or ten points if you chose A. This story is the true tale of a hoax: A botched April Fools' joke that went off a day early. Many drivers pulled over to watch the flying saucer maneuver through the sky and local residents called police to report the "alien invasion." However, the alien in the silver suit was Richard Branson, the chairman of Virgin records known for pulling pranks. Branson had had a hot-air balloon built to look like a UFO and set out to land it in London's Hyde Park on April 1. But the wind threw him off his flight path, forcing him to land in the wrong spot a day ahead of schedule.

Mermaid Makes a Splash, page 59

Give yourself five points if you chose B or ten points if you chose C. The mermaid was a completely bogus specimen made out of the body of a dead monkey and the tail of a fish. Crafty businessman P.T. Barnum dreamed up the hoax, got a long-time friend to pose as the English scientist, and billed the mermaid as a "Fejee beauty." Many critics declared it was fake and most viewers agreed it was extremely ugly. But that didn't stop people from lining up to see it. Exhibits of the Fejee Mermaid continued to sell out even years later after Barnum owned up to the hoax. And today, hoaxers still forge mermaids the same way. So remember this: There is no such thing as a mermaid!

If your score is between:

- 80 and 60, you're a Shrewd Hoax Buster. You know phony baloney when you see it. But you don't like to jump to any conclusions until you've considered all the facts and angles.

- 55 and 25, you're a Clever Hoax Buster. You like to size up the situation and examine the facts to draw your conclusions.

- 20 and 0, you're a Hoax Buster in Training. You jump to conclusions quickly. But if you slow down and give yourself time to go over all the facts and angles, you can become a Hoax-Busting ace.

Hoax Busters
How did you do?

Index